Mommy Blogging for Beginners

Table of Contents

Introduction

Money-making has become increasingly easier today – thanks to the internet, people, both young and old could now sit in the comfort of their living room, wearing nothing more than briefs, and earn as much money as they desire. Several online earning models are available, which the average person can leverage and create a consistent stream of income for him/herself. One of these online business models is blogging. Yes, you heard that right, BLOGGING.

People often think that blogging is an outdated way of making money on the internet – however, nothing can be farther from the truth. Blogging has been a viable way of making money online and will continue to be a significant online money spinner for those who know how to do it right. The problem when it comes to making money with blogging is that people are not willing to treat their blog like a business. Remember, anything that is not handled like a business will not pay you like a business.

If you want to be among those who are currently earning money from blogging, then this guide is for you. You might think that blogging is saturated but is there really any business in the world that is not saturated? Let's face it; every business you could think of is already saturated and what differentiates those who make it in one business from those who make excuses is the effort they put in.

One good thing with blogging is that if you put in the necessary effort and treat it like a business, it will pay you like a business. On the other hand, if you treat it like a hobby, it will cost you like a hobby. So, how do you create a blog and turn it into your personal cash cow? What type of blog do you need to create? What are the various blogging niches available to you? Ultimately, how do you run your blog like an actual business so that it can pay you like a business?

We will discuss all this and more in this all-encompassing guide. If you have been dreaming of earning money online through blogging, then join this ride. Even if you have been blogging for some time, but you have not recorded success, then it is evident that you are doing something wrong and we shall expose you to the right strategies that if you apply them, you will see your much-desired breakthrough.

Let's get started.

Chapter 1: Understanding Blogging

For a blogger, your foundation has two core components—who you're writing for and what you're writing about. In the rest of this chapter, I walk you through how to answer these two questions.

First thing is to think through your foundation-building process. Because if you don't get your foundation in place, your blog will have no clear direction and won't attract readers. Your readers are your potential customers. So, without readers, your chances of earning money from blogging will seriously diminish.

To make money from your blog, people must read it. So start thinking of who will read your blog and who are you writing for?

Don't say everybody. You cannot write content that appeals to everyone. It's not possible. There are millions of blogs online. If you try to attract everyone to yours, you will achieve the opposite.

No one will read it. They won't know why they should.

You must figure out who your ideal reader is. This is crucial, and it's a step I skipped with my first blog. I was writing for my family, but I also wanted to write about homesteading, homeschooling, and life in general.

I spent all my time writing for myself instead of for my readers. It's no wonder my blog didn't make any money for a long time.

I had no plan.

And as Benjamin Franklin said:

"If you fail to plan, you are planning to fail."

Don't plan to fail. Keep reading to learn how to identify an ideal reader for your blog.

WHAT ARE YOU GOING TO BLOG ABOUT?

Before picking an ideal reader, you need to know what you want to blog about. This is your niche. Here are ten popular, money-making niches:

> Blogging/making money online

> Personal finance

> Health

> Survival

> College prep/higher education

> Tech

> Personal development

> Lifestyle

> Food

> Fashion

Are those the only niches you can pick to make money? No! There are plenty of bloggers making money in other niches, like Jennifer Maker. Her crafting blog now earns a full-time income. So, don't feel limited by this list of niches. They're just some of the most popular ones, not the only choices available.

What are you passionate about? As you create content for your blog, you will dedicate hours of your life every month to this topic. It's a lot easier if you pick something you know about and care about.

To help you find your niche, get out a piece of paper and a pen. Spend a couple of minutes brainstorming topics you would like to write about.

When you finish, read over your list. Look for patterns. Do most of your topics fall under one main category? If so, congratulations. It looks like you have a starting niche.

If not, don't worry. Spend a little more time thinking. See if any of the ideas on your paper spark other topic suggestions.

Think about the topics your family and friends ask you for advice about. Are you the go-to computer gal who provides better service than tech support? Do you know a lot about troubleshooting car problems? Are you a master organizer? Do you enjoy repurposing old items into something beautiful?

Use your skills and interests to help you pick a niche for your blog.

THREE COMMON FEARS ABOUT PICKING A NICHE

It's common to feel nervous about picking a niche. I often hear people say:

1. I'm not an expert in any area.

2. What if I pick the wrong niche?

3. I have too many interests to pick just one.

People tend to use these excuses as a reason for not blogging. The fear of picking the wrong niche stops their progress completely.

Don't let fear stop you from starting.

FEAR #1: I'M NOT AN EXPERT

Contrary to popular belief, you don't have to be an expert at a topic to successfully blog about it.

You know why? Because even though a fourth grader doesn't yet know everything, a fourth grader is an expert in the eyes of a second grader.

You have knowledge. You have skills. You know more than some people. Your unique insight is valuable.

So, your goal is to write to the people who can benefit from what you offer. There will always be people who know more than you, or who do more than you. Those people are not your ideal audience.

But there are others who need you. Write for them.

FEAR #2: WHAT IF I PICK THE WRONG NICHE?

Picking the wrong niche is a very real possibility. You may not pick the perfect one right from the start. But if you don't start somewhere, you'll never get the opportunity to learn from the experience. Picking the wrong niche brings you one step closer to finding the right one.

Here are some warning signs you picked the wrong niche:

1. Your posts aren't getting shares, likes, or comments.

2. You don't enjoy your topic.

3. You can't easily brainstorm blog post ideas.

4. You can't find any other bloggers making money in the niche you selected.

These signs all indicate that you may need to tweak your niche. Listen to your audience and your gut, then start tweaking. Many successful bloggers shifted their focus over time when they realized what they were doing wasn't working anymore.

Alee King started The Beautified Life as a beauty and lifestyle blog, but she realized she didn't want to write about this topic forever.

Her true passion was in blogging and helping other moms create profitable blogs. She made the switch and her blog's stats and profits soared.

Your niche isn't set in stone. If you decide you picked the wrong one, shift your focus and pivot. You may lose some readers who decide they don't like the new direction you're taking, but that doesn't matter. Losing readers who are no longer in your target market is okay.

FEAR #3: I HAVE TOO MANY INTERESTS

Humans are beings with multiple passions. You have many interests and skills. The thought of picking just one feels limiting.

Don't worry that you're locking yourself in a tiny box by picking a niche. Your readers will want to get to know you. As you share your story and interests on the blog, you can offer insight into other aspects of your life, as well.

Perhaps you could add a "behind the scenes" post every Friday. Or publish a round-up post of items you love every other Tuesday. Don't be afraid to experiment. You can try something and see if your audience likes it or not.

Just make sure you aren't experimenting so often that no one remembers what the focus of your blog is.

In the introduction to this book, Sally shared how she struggled with having too many interests. Her solution was to find a common theme and write for one person.

CREATING YOUR IDEAL READER

Once you have a general idea of what you want to write about, it is time to figure out who your audience is. You need to create an ideal reader persona for your blog.

This step helps you get to know your readers. The more you learn about who is reading your blog, the more you can help them. And when you provide helpful content, you pull in readers who stick around and share your content with their friends and followers.

Before you make any more plans for your blog, or create a single piece of content, you need to nail down your ideal reader. Everything you do on your blog should speak to this reader.

Writing a blog post: Is it a topic your reader cares about?

Building a product: Does it solve a problem your reader struggles with?

Sharing a blurb on social media: Will the words and images resonate with your reader?

Creating a graphic: Is the style one your reader enjoys?

Recording a video: Does it speak to your reader?

Every aspect of your blog must work together for a single purpose: to serve your reader.

WHO IS YOUR IDEAL READER?

The more information you have about your reader, the easier it is to monetize your blog. As you think about your ideal reader, consider their characteristics. Here are five aspects to think about:

1. Demographics

2. Personality

3. Social habits

4. Media habits

5. Money habits

In the following sections, I dive deeper into each of these five aspects.

DEMOGRAPHICS OF YOUR IDEAL READER

Who is your ideal reader? Where do they live? What do they do? Demographics of your reader might include:

> Gender

> Age

> Location

> Level of education

> Income level

> Profession

PERSONALITY

The more you know about your ideal reader, the easier it is to craft content they will love. You need to dive deep into their personality. Here are some aspects of your reader's personality to consider:

> What are their interests?

> What do they do in their spare time?

> What prominent personality traits do they have?

> What are three adjectives used to describe this person?

> What are your reader's secret hopes and dreams?

> What would she most like to change about her life right now?

> What are her biggest problems or challenges?

> What keeps her awake at night?

> What kind of content would deliver exactly what she needs?

SOCIAL HABITS

Next, make sure you know where your ideal reader hangs out. Which of these networks does your reader use? How often are they on each?

> Pinterest

> Facebook

> Twitter

> Google+

> Snapchat

> YouTube

> Instagram

> LinkedIn

> Other

MEDIA HABITS

How will your ideal reader access your content?

> Which browser does your reader use?

> Do they favor a PC, tablet, or phone?

> Does your ideal reader prefer written, audio, or video content?

MONEY HABITS

Lastly, think about your reader's money habits. Here are some prompts to help you:

> What is your reader's relationship with money?

> What problems would they gladly pay for someone else to solve?

> What are your reader's favorite splurges?

> How does your reader primarily shop? (In the store? Online?)

> What stores does she frequent?

CREATING A PERSONA TAKES TIME

Answering all these questions about your ideal reader won't happen overnight. You may need to do some research, especially to learn more about social media use.

To research your audience, go where you think your target market is and start gathering data. Look at common questions on online forums like Quora. Check out questions in Facebook Groups or on other social media platforms. Read reviews of books you think your audience is reading on Amazon. See what information is missing, and what types of content they love.

If your friends are your idea reader, talk to them. Spend some time chatting about hopes, dreams, challenges, and habits. Listen and learn.

As you gather more information, use it to write down everything you can about your reader. The more details you capture, the better.

Naming your reader helps make them more personable. Then write a paragraph or two describing this person.

Chapter 2: Developing Killer Content

Setting up a blog using WordPress is a simple process that you can quickly learn on Google or YouTube. There are complete tools in WordPress that can be used to help set up a blog and creation of new content and posts. However, here are some tips that can make you an expert blogger and have more enriched experiences writing and publishing your thoughts online.

• Take a look at the plugins which are popular with bloggers. Research their efficacy and read the reviews of the bloggers on that plugin. It will keep you updated with the performance of your website as compared with others'.

• Keep your blog updated on a regular basis. It keeps your audience as regular visitors on the blog on one side, on the other, Google crawls it on regular intervals which increases the worth of your blog in search engines.

• Learn to write faster blog posts so that within minimum time, you can write more. There are some plugins to serve this purpose. You can upload them to improve the writing speed.

• Multi-author blogs are more influential. It creates better impression and diversity of thoughts on blog instead of having monotonous tone of words by one author.

• Answer the comments of those who visited your blog post and left their opinion on the topic you discussed in the post. Individually addressing those visitors will bring good will to you.

• Know your audience; their demand, expectations, possible responses or reactions to a particular thought you expressed in your post. Other features you should consider while posting are age, education, culture, mindsets, occupation, gender, income bracket, geographic zone, hobbies, and interests. It will help you write better and be understood in a better way.

•   Bring something unique and surprising in your blog posts. No idea or thought is absolutely unique. It is your words that will make it unique and impressive. Show your personality out of your words and make others feel the warmth and efficacy of your ideas. Words are the window towards your soul. Make this window attractive and opening new horizons of ideas and debates.

•   Keep the blog content unique. Never copy and paste the idea or words of someone else. It will damage the strength of your thought in the eyes of visitors on one hand and will decrease the rank and value of your blog in search engines on the other.

•   Make your share buttons smooth and active and share it on all Social Media icons regularly. It will make your blog an interactive community sharing thoughts with the like-minded people around the globe. Sharing buttons should be easy and in the right place to be shared by the readers using maximum icons including FaceBook, Twitter, Linkedin, Pinterest, Instagram, G+, and others.

•   Adopt an effective and multi-faceted approach to promote your blog. Promotion of the blog is equally necessary as the writing posts on regular basis is important. It is not an overnight process. It will take some time to be visible and popular but after getting popular, it will bring the fruits.

•   Make sure everything you post on your blog is true, not misleading or hurting anyone's thoughts, culture, and creed. You will be responsible for every word and image you post on it.

•   Make your blog attractive to look at. Its theme, colors, and face should be appealing to please the visitors. A beautiful but professional theme enhances the readership of your blog. Research the topic you are writing on. Proofread it before publishing.

Chapter 3: SEO

SEO (Search Engine Optimization) do you really know what the term means, and should you care about it if you have a blog that needs to be earning an income for you? These days blogging is a popular way to get before a global audience without breaking the bank, in this section we are going to look at what SEO can do for your online presence, the rationale of it and how to use it to your advantage, and also elude methods that could get your account blocked.

The phrase Search Engine Optimization (SEO) explains the route that affects your blog's status, in the blogosphere, i.e., the place it has on the ranking page when someone types in a search term.

For example, if you have a cake decorating business, and you also run a blog about the subject, when someone wants to order a fancy cake, your blog has to be optimized so that when someone writes in 'where to buy fancy cakes locally' into the Google search bar your blog should appear on page one of the search results at the number one spot. Keep in mind that Google is the largest and most used search engine in the world to locate services and businesses.

This imperative because it all about getting visitors to your blog so they can see what you are selling. You can always buy in traffic from a local web company to grow your customer base but don't do it till you know what you are paying for. The greater the traffic that comes to your blog, the better the opportunities that you will make sales. You want to make sure that you never leave the number one spot on page number one because you will get as much as sixty percent of the clicks in comparison to the rest of the results. It is also important to make sure that all your pages are up to speed because

Google grades singular site pages rather than complete blogs. Google sends robots to your page, and they follow orders! Again there are plugins to that can help with this.

Whether you are running a personal blog or a business blog, Google has an ever changing methodology or algorithm to ascertain the relevance of a page. Although Google can be quite transparent about sharing information as how it comes to a decision, much of it is shrouded in mystery, because they really don't want to share that kind of information in case people abuse it. All you need to know is how search engines work and to make sure they work to your advantage.

Your blog has to be relevant to what your message is all about. People come to search engines to look for something. It could be information, or they are looking to purchase an item. This next point is very important, make sure at all times that the methods you use to monetize your blogs are genuine and honest, because you don't want to be banned from Google. Trust is a very high issue with Google and almost impossible to get reinstated

Here is a checklist of things we need to consider in order to tell you if your site is search engine friendly:

On-site SEO

It must have original and applicable information. All your copy has to be highly fixated on the topic and not the keywords you are trying to rank for. These days you don't have to cram in keywords, you can be more selective in how you place them on your blog.

If you are unfamiliar with keywords there are many other blogs out there that can provide more information!

Closed Site SEO

Most sites have backlinks coming back to them and for Search Engine Optimization recognition. You can obtain backlinks by, writing observations or short content on those sites that include a connection to your site. Wait till you know what you are doing because the need to make sure that they are relevant to your niche and target market. As you get into the whole realm of blogging, you will discover many new techniques, most of them are usually free.

Chapter 4: Scheduling Your Blog Posts

When planning your blog content writing for your new online business, it can be difficult to come up with fresh new ideas. To develop an influential blog that attracts many visitors you need to be updating it consistently and habitually. This can be done by planning and organizing your posts through a schedule. You have probably come from that regimented environment where there has been rigorous scheduling and time management. This same regimen also applies to when you are writing a blog the only difference is that now you are working from home. You are probably groaning, but once the schedule is set up for your blog content writing and put into place, you'll realize how much easier it is to work.

Go ahead with the first task of deciding on a time for your blogging calendar. When you set up your first blog calendar choose a shorter period of a month or even a quarter.

Then formulate a list of topics that you want to discuss in your blog posts. When you are thinking of ideas here, put yourself in the shoes of your target audience and write on issues they might be keen to know about.

Once you have your list it is time to do keyword research to find out what phrases related to your topics are being searched for. Source out phrases which are being searched and which have a low competition for you to have a chance of competing against. There are many ways to to this but a great way is to use the Google Keyword Planner. I will not be going into depth with this but once again you can find plenty of resources online to learn this process.

Now pick the days when you will be publishing a blog post and record those on a calendar. Next, to each entry write in the title, the keyword phrase you will focus on, and a short summary of the topic you will write about.

To set up this schedule some outlay of your time will be necessary, but once you have done it, you will find that you get blog posts published more regularly and efficiently. When the time comes to write your blog post for that day, all the planning and preparation has been done, and all you need to do is write it out, it's that simple. Also, you are creating a log of ideas, and that is a good thing because you won't miss anything.

Managing and monetizing a blog is a big project, so if you break it into smaller more manageable action steps it will make the whole job of doing content writing more enjoyable.

Note:

Before you begin any project you must check out the competition because you need to know what you are up against. For Instance, you need to know how their site is designed, it's ranking in the search engines, branding, messaging, audience, products content writing, images, and promotions.

By taking a look "under the hood" you can also measure what initiatives they are undertaking by tracking their employment of optimization/testing tags, marketing and media, survey tools and social platforms. Once you begin to mind map the site, this is the time to take a look at your competitors' traffic and audiences and begin to understand how and what they are doing so you can do it better. Checking how long they have been in existence gives away a lot.

By researching your competitor's traffic levels and audiences you can measure the traffic you should be receiving, and your target audience. It is advisable to look at direct competitors and companies outside of your direct category and industry that are considered to be the best.

Chapter 5: Investing in Yourself

When you make the decision to start a blog, you are making the decision to invest in yourself. Whether you want to blog as a hobby, to connect with other bloggers, make a supplemental income, or eventually turn it into a full-time gig, you are essentially making the choice to build a brand. In order to do that, you need to invest in your blog the same way you would any other business.

After purchasing your web hosting and site domain, there are a few other things you may spend some money on in order to position yourself as a professional right out of the gate. While you're just starting out, it may also be a good idea to set a budget for your blog investments.

Here are some of the investments you may need to consider when starting a lifestyle blog:

Blog Design

Hiring a designer to spruce up the look and feel of your blog is something you may want to consider if you don't maintain any design or HTML skills yourself. The cost of a decent website design can range anywhere from $15-$500.

You may already know or have a connection with someone who is experienced in graphic and web design. If so, think about whether or not they would be a good fit for helping you design your blog and accomplishing the overall aesthetic you want to achieve.

If you don't have a designer in mind that you can hire to work on your website, I recommend searching Fiverr.com. It's a marketplace of independent freelancers. On Fiverr you can search for blog designs and templates. You can even hire designers through Fiverr to create a custom web design based on exactly what you're looking for.

Pre-made blog templates are available for purchase for as low as $15. Make sure you take note of which platform they are meant for. Some blog design templates are made specifically for WordPress, while others are made for Blogger or others. Also keep in mind: you get what you pay for. By sticking with a tighter budget, you may not get all of the extra gadgets and gizmos you wanted. It also won't hurt to start small and discover what you do and don't like before getting into the nitty gritty details. You can always change it later if you decide to. Design is not permanent.

If you're not sure where to start with blog design, ask around. There may be other bloggers in your network that can help by referring a friend or directing you to someone who knows a lot about design work. You can also ask for quotes and figure out what works best for your budget.

High Quality Photos

Part of being a lifestyle blogger means having great imagery included in your blog posts. After spending money on an attractive blog design, you'll most likely want to keep up the aesthetic appeal by posting high resolution photos.

Having great photos on your site will improve your blog's overall credibility on the Internet.

If you don't already have a DSLR camera, it may be time to consider investing in one. If you don't know much about photography and are on the fence about purchasing a camera, consider signing up for a photography class or searching for courses online. There are a lot of resources that can help you understand your camera and how to take the best possible photos for your blog.

Along with having the right camera equipment to ensure quality photos, you may also want to invest in some photo editing software. Adobe Photoshop and Adobe Lightroom come highly recommended in the blogging world and there are a lot of resources and tutorials to guide you through using them to make your photos look professional. By visiting Adobe.com and signing up for Adobe Creative Cloud, you can select individual apps to purchase. Adobe also offers different plans and bundles. Photoshop and Lightroom are only about $9.99/month, or you can purchase all of the Adobe apps for around $50/month.

If you don't have the budget to spend big bucks on expensive software, don't fret. There are several websites that let you perform simple edits to photos. Some of these sites charge a small monthly or yearly subscription fee to use more advanced filters and editing techniques. If this is more up your alley, give PicMonkey.com or Canva.com a try. They are very easy to use and can enhance the quality of your photos with just a couple clicks of your mouse. Keep in mind they aren't as advanced as some other software, but they'll get the job done if you're pinching pennies.

There's more to high quality photos than just expensive equipment and notable editing software. In order to have great photos, you typically have to know how to use a camera or have a photographer who can capture what it is you need. If you need someone to take photos for you, you won't just need a photographer, but you'll need someone who understands your style and is willing to work with you and your expectations for your blog posts.

It may come as no surprise that behind many style bloggers' photos is a significant other or spouse who is voluntarily helping the bloggers follow their dreams. Lucky for me, my husband, Steve, has always been a trooper about taking photos and taking the time to learn more about my camera and what its capabilities are.

Continuing Education

I don't mean "continuing education" in the way you might initially be thinking. This has nothing to do with college courses or receiving grades on how you perform as a blogger. This has to do with investing in yourself and learning from the best bloggers out there, and there's a simple way of doing that: conferences, workshops, summits, and panel events.

Now, I haven't been to many conferences or blog workshops, but I can tell you that one of the most effective ways to become a better blogger is by learning from others who have been around the block a few times. There are numerous blogging conferences that happen around the world throughout the year.

If you feel like a conference may be what you need to get started with a high-performing blog, then I'd recommend looking into ones in your area first, and then broadening your horizons. Blogging conferences can run anywhere from $500-$2,000, which usually don't include the cost of travel.

For a great list of different blogging conferences hosted throughout the year in different cities, check out "The Ultimate List of Blog Conferences" by Inspired Bloggers University.

There are also many different online services and educational courses that can teach you how to market your blog, monetize your blog, turn it into a business, write your own blogging book, and so much more. Don't be afraid to search the web for tutorials and online training for things that will benefit your blog.

Email Marketing Service

Another important investment to make in your blog is an email marketing service so that you can start to build your list. One of the single most effective ways to reach your audience is to show up in their email inbox when you share a new update.

If you think email marketing is dead, think again. Email is still super effective for a multitude of reasons. For one, it's personal and you just can't put a price on personalizing messages to your readers. It's also a direct form of communication to your audience without using a third party platform like Facebook or Twitter.

Your mailing list is what can give you a constant source of traffic to your website if you use it effectively. The more people subscribe to your list, the more likely you are to receive continued hits on your website.

Building an email list doesn't happen overnight, it's something bloggers continue to achieve day in and day out. It takes a lot of thought and planning to get hundreds of people to opt-in to your email list. Simply adding an email social icon to your blog's sidebar for people to follow you via email doesn't necessarily cut it in terms of growing a list.

Many online email marketing services guide you through different ways to build your email list on your website. The single best way to get users to subscribe is by offering an opt-in form directly on your homepage. These opt-in forms are also commonly referred to as lead magnets.

If you're starting a food blog, you can try using lead magnets like "10 Recipes with 10 Ingredients or Less" or "Download this Free Meal Calendar!" If you're starting a fashion blog, use lead magnets like "5 Different Body Types and How to Dress Them" or "Weekend Travel Checklist." If you're a travel blogger, effective lead magnets could be "The Weekend Travel Packing List." I think you're starting to get the picture.

Using an email marketing service takes a bit of investment, typically after you reach a certain number of subscribers on your list. Sites like Mailchimp.com and ConstantContact.com are user-friendly services that offer free trials. MailChimp is completely free until you reach over 2,000 subscribers, and Constant Contact offers a 60-day free trial period. So, fortunately for new bloggers, there isn't an initial charge. You can take some time, learn how to use the service, create some different opt-in options, and see how they perform before you decide on paying a monthly fee.

Once you have a decent list started, you can start creating different email campaigns or sending some premium content to all those who subscribe to your blog. It's important to make your subscribers feel special by offering exclusive bonuses that the average website visitor doesn't receive.

Having a mailing list is one of the most effective ways to drive traffic, increase engagement, and take your blog to the next level. Email is the most powerful way to communicate with your audience. You can be direct and to-the-point, while also offering high value content. You can even customize your messaging using personalization. It makes people feel important.

I didn't understand the importance of starting and growing a mailing list until just recently when I wanted to find unique ways to connect with my visitors. I spent several years completely missing out on tapping into opportunities to engage with others who actually wanted to hear from me.

How I Failed at Investing in Myself

I guess the easiest way to describe my initial failure with investing in myself was simply not investing in myself. I had little experience with how to use a camera properly, I knew nothing about how to design a website (or host one), I didn't have any previous knowledge of the blogging world other than what some close blogging friends had told me, and I definitely didn't have an email list or even know how to start one.

Starting out, the images I posted on my first blog were grainy at best. I knew little to nothing about taking high resolution photos, how to edit them, or even how to resize them using HTML. It wasn't until I started learning more about cameras in my film production classes that I realized I needed to get my act together and start coming off as a bit more professional. Soon after, I purchased my first DSLR camera and paid for an online training system recommended by a friend of mine called Photography Concentrate so that I could learn some basic photography skills. It was a total game changer to step back, start with the basics of understanding my camera, and learn how to best utilize light to get the most impactful photos for my blog.

I also completely failed to learn new and exciting things about the blogging world. Things like basic and advanced marketing tactics, creating meaningful and shareable content, and more. I learned over time (and the hard way), that I can't expect to become more knowledgeable unless I open up to the idea of being taught by some of the best. It is okay to invest in yourself. It's also a tax write-off, too.

I still continue to fail every day at building up an email list. To be honest, I really underestimated the power of growing a list until I saw how important and powerful it was for the company I currently work for. It's a bit advanced for anyone who wants to just get started with blogging, so I'll spare the details. What I will say, though, is learning about lead magnets, trip wires, and conversion funnels through Digital Marketer's DMHQ gave me the most incredible insight on the importance of just having a mailing list and what it can do for your blog and business growth.

Chapter 6: Making Money with Blogging

There's a very good reason why monetizing your readership is the very last step in this book about how to start a blog.

That's because today ... while you're just getting started, monetization should not be your #No.1 focus.

You need to find your readers, start building good relationships with them, forming a community around your blog, and keep delivering value (in the form of content) before immediately trying to sell them on an online course, buying your freelance services, or anything else.

Blogging is an investment that can pay enormous profits, however, it's a longer-term payout.

Indeed, even still, it's great to have a thought of which ways you'd like to make cash blogging as you go into this.

Presently, remember that when you're simply beginning, some of these monetization strategies will be easier than others while your readership is still developing.

In this section, I'm going to discuss all the aspects of how you can make money blogging.

1. CPC (Cost Per Click) ad Networks

In my 8 Year Blogging Journey, I used a lot of different CPC ad Networks on my blogs. The most profitable and successful one is Google's AdSense. It is a cost-per-click ad model, so I get paid whenever readers click on my AdSense ads . As you know google is very smart. Google's responsibility is only to show relevant ads according to your post content. It is actually a pretty well built system, and as a result it is the easiest and quickest ways that most bloggers make money from their blog. Also, AdSense delivers most of the relevant ads according to your post content, which can be quite beneficial and helpful for every reader.

As an example, if I write an article explaining what web hosting is, but don't mention where to host one, AdSense will likely display ads for places to host a website. So, if my user read that article explaining what web hosting is and interested to host a website, they'll likely click on that AdSense ad to host a website, and you will get paid from your blog contents. All the way, when AdSense ads are optimized correctly, they are a great way to make money blogging.

Some other CPC ad networks you can join also,

• 	Media.net

• 	Chitika.com

• 	Infolinks.com

• 	etc.

2. CPM (Cost Per thousand Impressions) ad Networks

CPM (Cost Per thousand Impressions) advertisements are another great way to earn decent money with your blog. While CPC ads pays you for every click , on the other hand CPM ad network pays you according to an amount of impressions received on an advertisement. At the beginning these CPM ad networks don't produce much income, but as the traffic grows on your blog, CPM networks seems to work well in combination with AdSense.

An "impression" means a single example of an advertisement appearing on your blog. This means that even if your readers aren't clicking the CPM advertisement, you'll still get paid.

Most of the CPM ad networks pay $1 to $10 for every thousands of impressions their ads get.

Some of the CPM ad networks which I used earlier:

- PropellerAds.com

- HillTopAds.com

- AdBuff.com

- Media.net

- Etc.

3. Freelancing (Selling Your Own services)

If you want to earn more from your blog, then selling your own freelance services is going to be your lowest effort option by far.

You need to set up a need a hire me page on your blog. You can sell your skills through your blog site like, design, article writing, web developing etc. There you must create 5-10 samples of your services and showcase them on your blog. As an example, if you're a Graphic Designer, you can create some demo designs and showcase them on your blog site.

If you do not have those sample demos yet... don't let that hold you back. Spend a few days right now to create those example articles, designs or other deliverables and host them on your own blog as if they were a project you got paid to produce.

If you have a skill that you can sell as a service, then you're already prepared to go out and start pitching potential clients. That skill could be something like...

- Article/Content Writing

- Graphic Design, Book Cover Design, Infographics Design

- Photography, Stock Photos Selling

- Web Developing, Web Designing

- Social Media Marketing, Digital Marketing, Content Marketing

- SEO or paid advertisements campaigns

- Business Strategy or Project Management

- And that list goes on... because any skills can be monetized.

Personally, I also sell my photography & content marketing skills. My first client paid me $200 for each article I wrote for their blogs. They found me through my blog, and liked the style of my blogs content, so it was an easy decision for them to choose me as a freelancer to increase their publishing at an affordable rate. So, try to find your skills to work as a freelancer.

4. Selling Digital Products

Today's world is all about digital products. Selling physical products, whether handmade by the designer or created by someone else, is highly changeable and extremely time-consuming. Also, there are a lot of complex things you have to take care of like shipping, international customers, taxes, laws, importing, inventory management and much more.

After the revolution of the web lot of traditional physical products are replaced by digital products. As an example, Traditional books are being replaced by Electronic Books (E-Book).

Selling digital products is very profitable due to not needing to pay unessential shipping fees, and other delivery problems on physical products and most importantly your customer can enjoy your digital product with just a click, no more waiting. You can also get same day feedback from your valuable customers.

Here are some of the most profitable digital products listed below:

1. E-Book:

Digital books or E-books have been and keep on being a standout amongst the most well-known digital products. They are moderately easy to deliver since they require no more than composed content and a couple of significant pictures. E-books are easy to circulate by means of huge commercial centers or self-made online stores. They're effectively devoured by clients, who can read them on e-readers, tablets, PCs, and even on their smartphones.

One of the best parts of making eBooks is that you can share nearly anything you know, or are passionate about and sell it on your site.

Advantages of EBooks:

*   Easy to Make

*   Easy to Sell

*   Clear Value Proposition

Disadvantages of eBooks:

*   Lots of Competition

*   (Almost) Saturated Market.

*   But you can rise if you work smarter.

2. Software:

Selling Software online is something we should know a considerable lot about. The software business is gigantic and reliably developing. Any individual's capacity to compose code of any sort can result in new, helpful items. Regardless of whether it be desktop software, online applications, site layouts, versatile web applications, computer games, or whatever else fueled by code. The outcomes are huge, and a market likely exists.

On the off chance that you talk (or rather, compose) a code language, you can build up various things to sell on the web.

Regardless of whether you have involvement with applications, modules, topics, pieces, sites, or something different altogether extraordinary, you can transform code into money.

Advantages of Software:

- Fulfills a specific function that people will be looking for

- Less Competition

- Easier to generate revenue

Disadvantages of Software:

- Creating code is difficult

- Have to provide ongoing support/updates

3. Online Courses:

E-Learning is an ever growing industry, and is developing with exceptional force. As it develops, we are beginning to see more and more courses at reasonable pricing being developed everyday. With respect to set up, online courses can be sold in a couple of ways:

- As a downloadable single course

- As a downloadable collection of courses

- As a membership/subscription to a web-based service.

Courses are sold in similar fashion as other computerized items, and with similar instruments, which is the reason we've turned out to be exceptionally acquainted with online course merchants.

A few courses are altogether self-sufficient, while others offer collaboration with an educator or task analyst. Numerous courses give understudies some type of affirmation or reward upon fruitful finishing.

Courses are turning into a well-known resource for online organizations, because of buyer patterns, and the pervasiveness of reasonable and simple to-utilize Learning Management Systems. They offer a worthwhile outlet for anybody with information or skill, and empower teachers to reach a large crowd without being compelled by geology, innovation or time.

Advantages of Software :

- Take Longer to create but provide more value

- Sell for higher prices

- Need high quality website if you use your own platform.

4. Other Selling Digital Products :

- Graphics/Digital Art

- Films

- Music

- Web Apps

- Subscriptions

- Private Memberships

- WordPress Themes/Plugins

- Artwork

- Photography

- Audio & Music

- Videos

- Documents

- Professional Services

- Fonts

5. Affiliate Marketing

If you do not have a digital/physical product to sell, then you can use the "Affiliate Marketing" model. Affiliate Marketing is another great profitable way to make money with your blog.

What is Affiliate Marketing?

Affiliate Marketing is Promoting someone else's product and getting a good commission for every sale.

As an example, if you join with XYZ affiliate brand to sell their product, they'll give you a unique tracking link. You then promote to targeted people who require that product & whenever people click and purchase from your unique link you'll get commission for those sales. (Commission can vary from platform to platform, starts from 2% and max upto 70%)

Mainly, it isn't much different from being a sales representative for an organization aside from that online you can do it for multiple organizations. As a result, you can earn a good amount of commissions from multiple resources.

There are millions of affiliate program options available on the Internet now. Some programs are listed below:

- Affiliate-program.amazon.com

- CJ.com

- Sharasale.com

- Clickbank.com

- Rakutenmarketing.com

There are many available, but these are the top ones.

You now got some affiliate programs but how do you promote them?

You can promote through your content. I have a very strong policy, give my readers the most honest recommendations. I give my honest opinion about the affiliate product to my users regardless of how it affects my affiliate sales.

For example, if you promote a product through your content which you know nothing about. Your readers spend money on that brand and they scam your readers. From that moment on your readers will never trust your word and will never recommend your blog ever. So, before promoting any product use that product and share all honest advantages and disadvantages of that product so that your readers can decide if that product is for them or not. Also, your readers will start to trust you.

In the blogging industry, for long term business, your #1 priority is to get readers to trust your content.

6. Direct Sponsor ad sales

Another monetization strategy is to sell ad space directly to advertisers. In certain niche blogging markets direct advertisement deals can work out great. With that being said, if this is a route your interested in taking, look at buysellads.com. This webpage is essentially similar to a go-between helping bloggers and sponsors get associated.

Bonus: How To make $10,000+ every month?

It is very possible to make $10,000 every month. Many bloggers out there do so every month!

After producing a digital product (eBook, video course, software or anything else) or having an affiliate product, you can make this $10,000/Month very easily.

If your eBook is priced between $2-5 and you have almost 5k per day targeted visitors on your site, you can make it very easily.

Suppose you have 10 high quality eBooks or video courses and every ebooks/video course price is between $2-5. Every day you're getting 5000 visitors and if 5% of them proceed with purchasing any of your ebooks then you will get 5000 * 5% = 250 sells every day. It means you will get $2 * 250 = $500 every day and $500 * 30 = $15,000+ every single month!

You can reach this figure only when you have good recurring traffic on your blog. Also, you need to imply many promotional strategies on selling your digital products or affiliate products via email marketing, google ad marketing, facebook marketing etc.

How Long does it take to make money from a blog?

Nearly everyone who creates a brand-new website for the first time asks this question. Well, let me tell you that if you're looking for a fast way to make money from your blog then blogging isn't it. It takes time and a lot of hard work behind a successful blog.

"Drive more Traffic to earn more"

I still remember those days when I started my journey towards blogging; I was checking my analytics every day. Each and every day I would sign into my analytics to check whether anyone had come to see my empty site.

It seems very silly, but it's actually a common practice for every newbie blogger. First six months I got zero sales and only a few visitors which were probably some of my school friends.

Do you want to know what happened next? I just focused on my content's quality. This is one of my favorite quotes in this business!

"Focus on quality, not quantity"

Also, I learned a lot of SEO practices and focused on creating more content so that my visitors will never feel bored and will never click on the close button after seeing my site. In other words, I focused on creating better user interface.

It was a long journey of learning what to do or not to do, sometimes failing but never giving up for a second. At first I didn't think much of making money because this mentality makes our thinking paralyzed. Give yourself time to create high quality content and think like a reader... What do your readers want to read?

Someone once asked me, why did you started blogging?

My answer was to help others and share all the advantages of a life full of freedom.

It may take a few months but whenever you learn all the techniques of SEO, Social Media Marketing, Building Backlinks, Attractive Content Marketing & other marketing techniques, you can earn money easily from your blog.

The two key components of blogging are Patience and willingness to learn

Without those key components it's hard to make money blogging.

6. How to Get Traffic to Your Blog

You have now built your first blog!

Now, how do you drive traffic to your blog?

If you think that people are automatically going to swarm your blog, Sadly your wrong. People won't discover your blog (at the beginning anyway) except if you complete a little legwork. These are a few of the things I did to get traffic and some that I still do.

1. Produce High Quality and Unique Content

I know this is sounding repetitive at this point but if you want to rank on the search engine, then you need to produce high quality and unique content. This is one of the most noteworthy tips of all but there are few bloggers that actually follow it.

Try to provide in-depth information-rich, keyword-rich and useful content that could be helpful for readers and search engine bots to find you quickly. Owning an extensive, well structured, high-quality unique site is a very solid investment for your future.

Google has confirmed that without quality content websites will not rank well on the search engine.

After all, if you write useful content that helps people then they will love your blog and also remember it for future visits.

2. Use a Reliable Web Hosting

It's very important to use a reliable Web Hosting service like, Bluehost to increase more organic traffic.

While crawling search engine bot, if your site is down then your site will never rank well on search engine. So, You need a reliable Web Hosting which have minimum server downtimes.

If you have a bunch of sites, I strongly recommend you use quality web hosting platforms to reduce possible server downtime. If you are using popular Web Hosting Providers like Bluehost or Hostgator you should see minimum downtime if any at all.

3. Keep Adding New Content

According to Google, half of the 3 billion organic searches done a day in Google are for unique keywords, because people want to know about new things.

You have to find those unique keywords to start writing on those Unique topics.

Search engine's rank websites higher who are naturally adding new content which is unique from others.

If people want to know about that unique content, they can find your unique content on the first page of google or any other search engine.

When you're adding new content, you must remember to post it on a regular schedule so search engine bot remembers your presence.

I recommend you post a minimum of 1 article per week, 2 is preferable, adding an article daily is very good and adding 1 every 8 hours is outstanding but not necessary to rank on search engines

4. Choose a memorable domain name

If you're launching a new blog/website then your domain name must be short and memorable so that visitors remember it.

Try to choose a domain name which won't confuse people with other similar names to your competitors. You don't want to people visiting your competitor's domain name when they want to visit on your site.

NameBoy.com is a handy tool that you can use for searching your memorable domain name.

5. Purchase the Wrong Domain Name as well.

If you think people may confuse your domain name with a similar name then you can purchase the wrong domain names too.

As an Example, you know about Facebook.com, they also bought a few wrong domain names to help people finding their destination. if you search with facebooks.com, it also redirects to facebook.com.

It means Facebook knew that people can misspell facebook.com so they bought the other domain facebooks.com to help people find their website.

Moreover, it also helps Facebook to generate more traffic.

Also, you can buy other extensions like, .net, .org etc with your domain names.

6. Keyword Research to increase Free Organic Traffic

If you want to get more free Organic traffic from search engines then you need to find out the exact keywords which most people are searching for.

There are free and paid tools available for finding keywords. But, I will recommend you to use Paid tools like SEMrush to get more long-tail keywords which helps you to drive more Organic traffic on your blog.

With over 35 + tools and 9.4 billion keywords, SEMrush is a paid subscription and it is used by thousands of professionals worldwide. SEMrush is the best SEO tool for WordPress because of its 24/7 customer service.

With SEMrush you also can find your competitors strategy on building links, focusing keywords, your sites organic keyword position, ideas for getting more organic traffic and lots more features.

7. Improve Page Titles and Meta Description

Page Titles are one of the most important factors to attract your visitors.

First, Go to Google and research your keywords and look at the Top 10 search results.

Now you can see every web page has a unique title and meta description.

This gives you an idea of what eye catchy titles and meta descriptions your competitors are using.

Now go to your site and edit your site title and meta description with a more eye catching title and description.

Try to implement focus keywords on title and meta description to increase rankings and organic traffic from search engines.

8. Blog Commenting

One of the definite great ways for new blogs to get traffic is just to comment on other high DA (Domain Authority) & PA (Page Authority) sites. You must remember to comment on related niche of your own blog. Commenting with a thoughtful as well as provocative reaction will frequently send some traffic to your blog. The blogging network is generally extremely social, and those who are dynamic, regularly receive the benefits. But more significant than the couple of guests you get from it is the relationship you can create with different bloggers.

I just read other blogs and try to contact them through the comment section. If I love their content then I leave a comment telling them how much I appreciate their content, as well as any mistakes I may find. This is a great way for you to get recognized and earn trust from other audiences. This is one of my favorite ways to get traffic sent to my blog. The important part is not to sound like you are only there to try and attract their audience. It is important to provide value first. Then you can suggest your blog.

9. Submit to Directories

The more high-quality backlinks you have the better you will do on search engines.

Here are some of the best directories where you can get backlinks.

- botw.org

- aboutus.com

- blogarama.com

- Submit Your Site on Google My Business

- Submit on Bing Places

- Submit on Yahoo

- Brownbook

- Yelp

- Foursquare

- elocal

- Yellowpages

- Hotfrog

- SuperPages

- Alignable

- local.com

- MerchantCircle

- B2B Yellow Pages

Be sure to read the submission rules before submitting your site on these above directories.

10. Submit Articles Via Email Newsletter

This is another good method to get a lot of free traffic on your site.

I always recommend to capture your visitor's emails and promote your content to get a lot of free traffic from email marketing.

If you can build a relationship with your visitors via email marketing then you will get a lot of recurring visitors on your site.

So, always try to build a list of good visitors who need your service.

11. Linking to Other Blogs

This is another way to build your link from high authority sites. When people link to my blog I get notified and I try to find their content. If it is high quality and I believe it to be valuable to my readers then I share on my social media sites. This is another great way to reach people through the pros. You can also mail them after linking content and let them know you loved their content and shared it with your audience. This may get them to read your content and link back to your blog. Many bloggers use this trick and, in this way, get high authority backlink.

12. Share on Social Media Sites

Sharing each and every post on social media is another great method to get your posts out potential readers and attract more organic traffic to your blog.

Social Sites like Facebook, Twitter, Pinterest, etc allow you to link to your site's content. So, always share on social media sites and try to suggest people check out your site for more at the very end of your post. Here is an example,

"If this post was helpful, you can also share this post on social media sites. Every share encourages me to write more about hidden facts. Visit XYZ.com for more great posts."

Every Social share allows your site to be more trustworthy for Search Engines, which increase your site's Organic Traffic.

13. Be helpful in Forums

Forum Commenting is another effective way to get targeted visitors. Getting involved with Forums or message boards related to your niche and having a link to your blog in the signature line can send a couple of visitors your way.

I follow a rule of helping others because this rule helps me get most of my followers. I love to write useful content for them and you can do the same to attract loyal followers.

At first, join a forum and post on a topic that you know most and try to research if that post was posted by any member before or not so you can give them a full informative article about that post.

Once you get a few follower messaging or trying to know about another topic you can link them directly to another post on your site.

Do a search in Google to find forums in your niche,

- yourkeyword + forum

- yourkeyword +"message board"

Remember don't spam, just provide value and if they like what you have they will follow you.

14. Start Podcasting to Drive more Free Traffic

Podcasting is another option to scale your blogging business to the next level.

You can start your podcasting on Youtube and Vimeo to get more free traffic on your site.

Start with in depth but short videos that may be helpful for your visitors. By podcasting you can also connect with other like-minded people.

I will recommend you to start with an introduction video on a feature page so that new people can understand your youtube channels topic.

15. Remove Broken Links

Removing all unwanted junk files can increase your operating system faster than previous. Similarly, removing all broken links can help you to increase organic traffic from search engines.

Search engines do not like broken or dead links so try to check every month if there are any links that are not working.

why don't search engines like broken links?

Search engines want to rank only high quality posts or pages so if there are any broken links, search engine bots crawl and get 404 errors it detects your post as not a quality post or page.

What you can do?

Don't Worry, just install a broken link checker plugin on your WordPress. It will take care of all broken links, just check every month to stay updated.

Conclusion

No matter where you are in your blogging journey, whether you're a beginner, intermediate, or advanced blogger, I hope you found something of value in this book. I hope we were able to help you to improve and monetize your blog.

If you liked this book and found it valuable, I would really appreciate it if you left an honest review of this book.

I wish you the best of luck on your blog, and hope that you find a phenomenal level of success with it!

Anna Harrison